# Old Japan

## 50 stress relieving designs

### by

### Jack Bajesi

# COPYRIGHT NOTICE

# INTRODUCTION

"Ukiyo is a genre of Japanese art which flourished from the 17th through 19th centuries. Its artists produced woodblock prints and paintings of such subjects as female beauties, kabuki actors, scenes from history and folk tales, travel scenes and landscapes" (Wikipedia)
This book contains 50 stress relieving designs obtained from nineteenth century Japanese prints and paintings found in the Library of Congress.

Owl and magnolia

Early spring

A young dandy and a woman on a veranda

An inn at Hakone

Five pines Onagi canal

A parody of the play Mount Kurama

Armor Hanging Pine

Actor in the role of Saitogo Kunitak

Asakusa ricefields and torinomachi festival

Public bathhouse where several women are bathing 1

Cherry viewing at Gotenyama 1

Brazier

Fuji hawks and eggplants

Mishima

Viewing cherry blossoms at Ueno 1

A procession of flowers before Mount Fuji

Indoor scene with several women **1**

Grandfather's teahouse, Meguro

Cherry viewing at Gotenyama 2

Yoshida

Public bathhouse where several women are bathing 2

Viewing cherry blossoms at Ueno 2

Woman arranging blossoming branches

Evening glow at Ryōgoku Bridge

Mokubo Temple

November

Fireflies

Flourishing fireworks at Ryōkoku Bridge Kawabiraki

Yanone gorō

Woman carrying a child on her back

Scene from a Soga play 1

Totsuka

Mid-Autumn

Rain in May

Cooling off near the river bank

The courtesan Takao of the Miura-ya

Nihonbashi clearing after snow

Scene from a Soga play 2

Minazuki

The armonic couple

Correspondence of Rajōmon

Indoor scene with several women 2

Geisha and a servant carrying her koto

The courtesan Suminoto of the Ōkana-ya

Snow

Itsutomi

Actor in the role of the Kokingo.

Princess Sotoori catching a spider with a fan

Actor in the role of Taheiji

Viewing a peep box show